W9-BTO-870

WATCHING NATURE

THE
LIVING
TOWN

Nigel Hester

FRANKLIN WATTS
New York/London/Toronto/Sydney

First published in the United States in 1992 by
Franklin Watts, Inc.
95 Madison Avenue
New York, NY 10016

Library of Congress Cataloging-in-Publication Data

Hester, Nigel S.
     The living town / Nigel Hester.
         p.   cm. — (Watching nature)
     Includes index.
     Summary: Describes the different kinds of plants and animals that
can be found in urban areas.
     ISBN 0-531-14202-7
     1. Urban ecology (Biology)—Juvenile literature.   2. Urban fauna—
Juvenile literature.   3. Urban flora—Juvenile literature.
     [1. Urban ecology.   2. Urban animals.   3. Urban plants.]   I. Title.
II. Series.
QH541.5.C6H47   1992   91-34488
574.5'268—dc20   CIP   AC

Editor: Su Swallow
Design: Edward Kinsey

Illustrations:
Angela Owen, Ron Haywood
Picture research: Sarah Ridley
Phototypeset by Lineage Ltd, Watford
Printed in Belgium

Photography:
Heather Angel 13c, 27tl; Bruce Coleman Ltd 4t, 6t, 10bl, 11b, 14b, 15br, 17tr, 18
(inset), 20br, 21tr, 23tl, 23b, 24c, 27tr, 27b, 28t; Nigel Hester 5b, 8t, 12t (inset), 13tl,
15tr, 15cl, 18t, 18b, 20c, 22b, 26t; Frank Lane Picture Agency 7, 7t (inset), 9tr, 11tl,
11c, 12t, 19tl, 19tr, 20t, 20bl, 21b, 22t, 23tr, 26b; Eric and David Hosking 13tr, 16bl;
Natural History Photographic Agency 5t, 5 (inset), 10t, 10br, 11c, 12b, 14t, 16t, 16br,
17b, 17c (inset); Oxford Scientific Films Ltd 4bl, 4br, 6b, 7b (inset), 8cr, 8cl, 8b, 9tl, 9b,
12 (inset), 15tl, 17tl, 21tl, 24t, 24b, 25 (both); Survival Anglia 6 (inset), 11tr, 13bl.

Front Cover:
Robert Harding Picture Library (main picture), Oxford Scientific Films Ltd (inset right),
Survival Anglia (inset left).

CONTENTS

WHAT KIND OF TOWN?

Do you live in a town or a city? Are the buildings mostly old or new? Is your town near the sea or the countryside? This book tells you about some of the wildlife to look out for in your town. The plants and animals you find will depend partly on where your town is and on the kinds of buildings there are. You will find more wildlife in towns and cities that have open spaces and water, but a surprising number of plants and animals have adapted to living right in the city center.

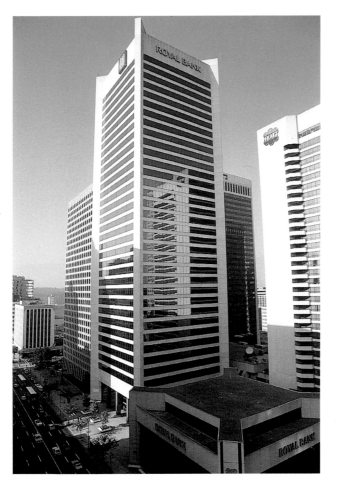

Rivers *(above)* can support all kinds of fish, birds, water insects, and plants, provided the water is not polluted. Modern towns *(left)* have less wildlife than old places *(below)*. New buildings of concrete, glass, and steel provide little food or shelter, but some birds nest on tall buildings.

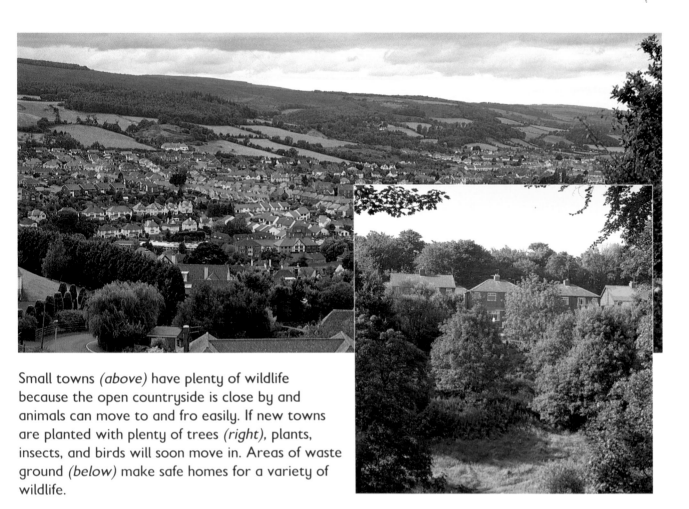

Small towns *(above)* have plenty of wildlife because the open countryside is close by and animals can move to and fro easily. If new towns are planted with plenty of trees *(right)*, plants, insects, and birds will soon move in. Areas of waste ground *(below)* make safe homes for a variety of wildlife.

Some towns and cities are very old. Plants and animals have had plenty of time to become established in these artificial environments. Wildlife continues to adapt as the towns grow and change. Parks, gardens, and golf courses form islands of countryside in towns. Rivers, canals, and reservoirs provide freshwater habitats for plants and animals. Dumps, landfills, empty lots, and disused buildings allow wildlife to flourish, with little disturbance from people.

LIVING CLOSE TO PEOPLE

At night, when most people are asleep, many animals are moving about in our towns. Some of them, such as raccoons and opossums, are surprisingly large, but they may be harder to spot than small ones such as rats, rabbits, and bats. All these animals live in urban areas as well as in the country. Many of them feed at night and rest during the day.

Rabbits need plenty of grass to eat. You may see them at dawn or dusk feeding in parks or in large gardens. Black and brown rats will eat almost anything, but black rats prefer fruit and brown rats like to eat cereals. Urban raccoons often overturn garbage cans and spread litter in their search for food.

△ Rabbits live in burrows. The best time to look for them is in May or June.

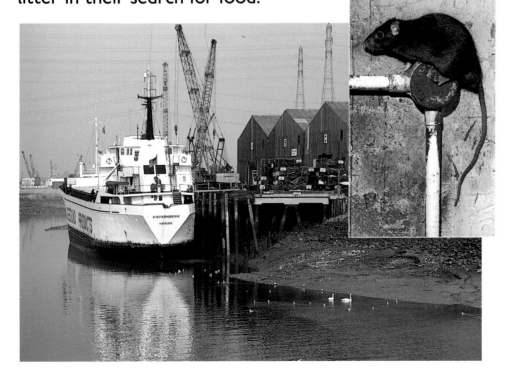

▷ In Britain, foxes live in many towns and cities *(main picture)*. They take food scraps from garbage cans and dumps. If pigeons are plentiful, foxes will eat them. Almost half the diet of young town foxes is made up of pigeons.

Pipistrelle bats *(inset, top)* live in colonies in the roof space of buildings.

Deer *(inset, bottom)* may visit backyards.

◁ Black rats *(inset)* are excellent climbers. They live in the rafters of buildings in ports *(main picture)*. Their droppings can spoil food kept in warehouses.

LIFE IN THE PARK

Town parks play a vital role in reducing air pollution. The trees and shrubs absorb some of the dust and fumes from vehicles, and trees help to deaden the noise of traffic.

The best parks for wildlife are those that are not disturbed too much. Few wildflowers or insects can survive in grass that is often cut short. Corners of parks that are left untouched are better for wildlife than very tidy areas. Native shrubs support more insects than do shrubs that come from other countries.

△ Ornamental shrubs from other countries are attractive, but may not support much wildlife.

▷ The candle-shaped flower of the horse chestnut tree attracts many insects.

Town pigeons (above) are common in parks, and flock to anyone who offers them food. Town pigeons usually nest on buildings, but many other birds build their nests in trees in parks. The horse chestnut (right) is often planted in parks and along wide streets.

The thrush *(above)* is commonly found in parks where it nests high in trees. It feeds on insects, snails, and berries. The wren *(left)* nests in bushes and hollows in walls. Wrens huddle in groups in winter to keep warm. The crow *(below)* can be a pest in parks, where it feeds on the eggs of water birds.

Native trees such as oaks and maples support a wide range of wildlife, and trees and shrubs provide nesting sites for many different birds. Old tree stumps and fallen logs are good places to find mosses, ferns, beetles, and wood lice.

Many parks have areas of open water. Ponds and lakes provide a home for many creatures. Ducks, geese, and swans may live on the water, insects visit the marsh plants that grow at the water's edge, and frogs and newts breed in the water.

Birds and small mammals visit zoos to find food and shelter. The caged animals leave scraps of food on the ground, which are soon devoured by starlings, crows, chickadees, and finches. People who visit the zoo also drop food, which the birds then eat. Ducks and geese often use lakes that have been created for exotic birds such as flamingoes.

Small mammals such as mice and rats can become pests in zoos because they steal so much of the food that is fed to the zoo animals.

△ Zoos are built mainly to keep wild animals in captivity, but zoos attract many native wild animals that are looking for food. Some of these animals, in turn, provide a meal for birds of prey such as owls.

△ Some wild birds collect the hair and fur from captive animals and use it as nesting material.

◁ Gray squirrels are regular visitors to zoos and parks. They take food from people, and hunt through litter baskets for tidbits.

△ Owls (*top left* adult, *above* young) sometimes nest near zoos and in parks. They feed on mice and other small mammals.

Lakes and ponds attract dragonflies (*above* southern hawker, which breeds in marshy vegetation). Coots, mallard, and swans (*right*) sometimes join exotic birds on the water in parks and zoos.

In any town or city there are always empty lots. Some plants and small creatures are quick to colonize these areas. Annual plants that grow and die in one season are the first plants to appear. They produce many seeds and spread easily. If the ground lies abandoned for several years, a succession of different plants will become established. Even tree seedlings will grow if left undisturbed. Ailanthus, for example, often sprout up in nooks and crannies between buildings.

In Europe after World War II, rosebay willow herb quickly colonized the bomb sites. It was nicknamed "fireweed" because it thrives on land covered in ash from fires, and is now common in vacant lots. The plant attracts many insects.

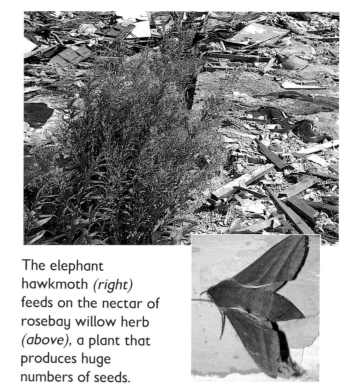

The elephant hawkmoth *(right)* feeds on the nectar of rosebay willow herb *(above),* a plant that produces huge numbers of seeds.

Buddleia *(right)* is quick to colonize waste corners *(inset).* It attracts bees, hoverflies, and butterflies *(shown here:* peacocks and small tortoiseshells). Buddleia, or the butterfly bush, comes from China, but although it is not a native plant it has spread rapidly and insects have adapted to feeding on it.

△ The stinging nettle has stinging hairs and greenish flowers that hang down. It is common in vacant lots.

(top right) Some birds take advantage of the peace and security of wasteland to raise their young.

The garden tiger moth *(above)* lays its eggs on nettles, on which its caterpillars *(left)* feed.

▷ The zebra spider can often be seen lying in wait for its prey on walls in towns.

Cemeteries in towns and cities, especially untidy ones, can be very rich in wildlife. The soil in cemeteries is often rich in lime, from the church building and tombstones, which encourages plants such as orchids and cowslips to grow. The soil may also be rich in calcium, from the bones in the ground, so calcium-loving plants such as stinking iris and quaking grass thrive.

Insects, snails, and slugs in the grass make easy meals for slow worms, mice, and voles. These animals, in turn, are hunted by owls and foxes. Moles are also quite common underground in cemeteries, where they feed on the abundant supply of worms.

△ Cemeteries are like tiny islands of countryside in towns and cities.

◁ Tunneling by moles, worms, and rabbits sometimes causes the ground to sink, which makes tombstones lean over at different angles.

◁ Red campion grows in shady spots in rich soil. Its flowers may be bright pink or quite pale.

▷ The ox-eye daisy is common in the grass of town graveyards.

▽ Lichens growing on tombstones can be very colorful. The oldest stones have the most lichens.

Yew trees *(below)* are often planted close to churches. They provide good nesting sites for birds, which feed on the red berries *(right).*

Lichens are common on stonework in cemeteries. They are very sensitive to pollution in the air. Fewer lichens can grow in large towns — where pollution is high — than in smaller, cleaner towns. Limestone tombstones support orange, yellow, or white lichens. Green powdery lichens grow on acidic stones. Droppings from birds that perch on the stones provide extra nutrients for the lichens to grow.

You might not expect to find much wildlife beside the road. However, the shoulders of wide roads and highways support a surprisingly large population of plants and animals. The grassy edges of highways are usually left undisturbed by people. Long grasses and flowers hide voles, shrews, and mice. The kestrel, a bird of prey, has quickly learned to hunt over these grassy shoulders. It has excellent eyesight and can spot the smallest movement as it hovers above the traffic. Other birds feed on the remains of animals killed by cars.

△ Wildflowers, such as these blue cornflowers, can grow beside busy main roads, if the grass is not cut too often.

▽ The kestrel *(below left)* is the commonest day-flying bird of prey in Britain. It lives on farmland, moorland, and along sea cliffs, and now even nests and hunts in the center of towns. Magpies *(below)* and crows are scavengers. They scour the roads looking for the remains of rabbits and other animals killed by the traffic.

The field vole *(right)* helps to spread the seeds of wild-flowers, which it carries on its body. Butterflies *(below, small white)* are attracted to the flowers on roadside shoulders.

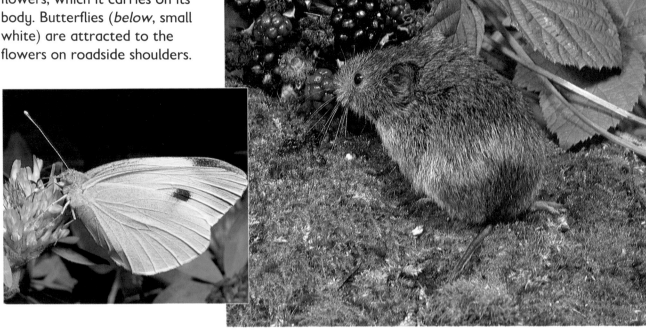

The London plane tree *(below)* is often planted beside roads in towns and cities. It rids itself of dirt by shedding its bark in great scales *(right)*.

Plants that grow beside the highway have to withstand toxic fumes from vehicle exhausts, together with oil, rust, dust, and rubber particles. Many survive and even flourish, despite this pollution. Some road shoulders have been colonized by coastal grasses that usually grow in salty soil by the sea. The grasses can grow inland where salt has been spread on roads to stop ice forming.

In town centers, roadsides may be planted with trees. The tree roots are covered by the pavement and road, yet they survive surprisingly well. Their flowers attract night-flying insects such as moths.

Plants and animals can live close to the railroad line with little interference from people, because cuttings and embankments are not open to the public. Such areas are often all that remain of the natural countryside that has been lost as towns and cities have spread.

Primroses, milkweeds, asters, and daisies all add color to the rich plantlife beside the track.

Some plants are even able to colonize the dry, stony area between the railroad tracks. Some are coastal plants that moved onto the track when pebbles were brought from the coast as ballast beneath the rails.

△ The sweet pea often adds a bright splash of color beside railroad tracks. It is a climbing plant that has spread to vacant land from gardens.

▽ The biting stonecrop grows in clumps, close to the ground. It thrives in bare, dry places and may be found between the railroad tracks.

△ Some animals can live close to the railroad line. Lizards *(above)* and slow worms like the dry conditions among the stones of the track.

Garden spiders *(above right)* hunt among the vegetation beside tracks and on other wasteground.

▷ Railroads have helped to spread plants throughout the country. The tiny spores (like seeds) of ferns, and light seeds from flowers may be carried many miles in the slipstream of a moving train. In this way ferns and other plants have colonized the damp brickwork of stations, bridges, and tunnels.

mosses

bladder fern

liverworts

rusty-back fern

Remember: do not walk beside railroad tracks.

Garbage dumps are usually found on the edges of towns and cities. Piles of food scraps, old paper, and other refuse on dumps have provided a new habitat for wildlife. Many creatures have adapted well to it.

One of the first birds to take advantage of garbage dumps, near the sea or inland, is the sea gull. Other scavengers that regularly feed on people's garbage include crows, starlings, rats, and mice. These animals also feed on the large numbers of insects and other small creatures that live on the dump. Springtails are tiny wingless insects that live in soil, leaf litter, and refuse. They usually move by walking, but they can jump out of the way by straightening out the "spring" that is held folded under their body.

△ Noisy seagulls are common visitors to dumps.

▷ Tough perennial plants such as the broadleaved dock can thrive on dumps.

▷ Springtails are found in damp places; they dry out easily.
▽ Bluebottles and other flies abound on garbage.

△ Crickets look like grasshoppers, apart from two or more "tails" which probably detect air movements and sound. House crickets (above) like the warmth of dumps.

◁ The spotted fly-catcher has no spots, except when it is young.

▽ The tail of the brown rat is nearly as long as its body.

In Britain, the number of flies around garbage dumps has attracted a shy bird normally found in parks and gardens, the spotted flycatcher. It feeds almost entirely on flies, which it catches when flying. The bird sits on a lookout post until an insect comes close, and then returns to the same post to await the next meal.

Rats are commonly found around garbage dumps. They feed on food waste at the dump, around picnic areas, and even in park litter bins. They are more active at night so are not usually seen during the day.

HIGH-RISE LIFE

The buildings that make up our towns and cities provide homes and places of work and leisure for people. However, to many kinds of wildlife these buildings are good substitutes for natural habitats. Tall office blocks and warehouses are treated as inland "cliffs" by some kinds of bird. The pigeon, for example, has evolved from the rock dove, which lives on rocky coasts. The pigeon roosts and nests on tall buildings. Herring gulls also nest on tall buildings. Urban gulls usually breed more successfully than their coastal relatives.

▽ Tall buildings *(below)* provide roosting and nesting sites for birds such as the pigeon *(bottom).* This pigeon's plumage is very variable: it may be blue-gray, brown, black or white, or any combination of these colors.

△ Starlings roost on buildings.

◁ Some plants are able to grow in the mortar of old walls.

▽ The peregrine falcon used to be common in many cities. Poisoning reduced its numbers, but it is now returning in some places, where it nests on buildings.

As the sun sets in many large towns and cities, the twittering and chattering of huge flocks of starlings may be heard above the noise of the traffic. Starlings, and pigeons, gather together on the ledges and sills of buildings to roost for the night. Their droppings may cover the stonework of the building and are difficult to remove.

The walls of older buildings are sometimes colonized by plants. They grow by pushing their roots into the soft mortar between the bricks.

People have always used rivers and the sea to transport goods. This is one reason why towns and cities have grown up beside rivers and the sea, and canals have been dug. In the past, rivers in major cities have been polluted by industrial waste. In recent years, the pollution has been controlled and rivers are becoming cleaner. The wildlife that was threatened is returning to the rivers.

Gravel pits are often dug on the edge of urban areas. Once abandoned, they fill up with water and provide valuable freshwater habitats close to town centers. Gravel pits and reservoirs are visited by many birds, especially during migration in the spring and autumn.

△ Rivers in towns provide a freshwater habitat for all kinds of plants, fish, birds, and other creatures.

▽ The goldeneye visits Britain in the winter and feeds on shellfish and water insects.

◁ Once filled with water, old gravel pits quickly become colonized around the edges by marsh plants such as reedmace, and eventually by water-loving trees.

▷ Swans (inset) often breed on rivers right in the center of towns and cities. Ducks, grebes, and many other birds nest among the vegetation (main picture, bulrushes) that grows at the water's edge on rivers, gravel pits, and reservoirs.

Most urban wildlife has moved into the human-made environment from the surrounding countryside, and has adapted to the artificial habitat. Most of the animals that live in or visit the places where we live are familiar to us. Sometimes, though, we may see some unusual or unexpected wildlife in our towns. It may be an animal that is normally kept in captivity, but has escaped into the wild. Or it may be a plant or animal from another country.

Sometimes these strangers in town are able to adapt to their new home and may quickly spread.

△ These bees have escaped from a bee hive and will establish themselves as a wild colony.

◁ Pets such as hamsters sometimes escape into the wild.

▽ Millet often grows on garbage dumps, from imported birdseed.

△ Cats that now live in the wild are called feral cats.

◁ The green tree frog from South America now lives in some towns in Europe.

▽ Cockroaches have spread to other lands with exported fruit.

Private gardens, botanical gardens, and parks contain many exotic plants. These plants may spread into the wild when seeds are spread by the wind or by animals. Birdseed mixtures contain seed from all over the world, and any seed that is thrown away will try to grow.

Ships often bring small creatures to our ports from other countries. Scorpions, unusual species of spiders and beetles, and even tiny tree frogs have arrived in this way.

Many towns and cities have their own urban nature reserves. They are areas that are set aside to develop naturally, and are protected from building development. If you have a nature reserve near you, you can visit it to find out about the wildlife that lives in your town. You may also like to volunteer to help look after the plants and animals in the reserve.

Many urban areas have their own wildlife group, which is a club for people who are interested in the wildlife in their town or city. You could join a wildlife group and help to protect the plants and animals in your area. Some groups design nature trails that link up important wildlife sites in city centers. Try following an urban nature trail to see local wildlife.

More and more trees are being planted in towns and cities. The trees are not only pleasant to look at, they also help to absorb some of the pollution in the air. See if you can find any newly planted trees in your area. How many different kinds can you find? You could draw a map of your area by copying a street map, and mark the trees on your map. You could add other plants and any wild animals that you spot as you walk about near your home.

△ One of the best ways to learn about wildlife in your town or city is to join a local club. These people are clearing scrubland.

Did you know?

 Adult foxes take toys back to their den for the cubs to play with. Tennis balls, rubber balls, and even golf balls have been found in dens.

 The black rat carries a flea that can transmit disease to people. The Great Plague of London in 1665 was caused by black rats. It killed many thousands of people.

 In Asia, monkeys and bats live inside temples in towns and cities.

 In the town of Churchill in Canada, polar bears regularly feed on tidbits from the garbage dump.

 In Africa, jackals, hyenas, and warthogs all visit towns to scavenge for food around buildings and on dumps.

Where to look for wildlife

Vacant land is quickly colonized by plants, which in turn provide food and shelter for insects, birds, and other small animals.

Walls and roofs of buildings may support lichens and other plants, and ledges provide ideal roosting places for birds.

Roadside and highway shoulders, and railroad embankments are often undisturbed by people, so wildlife can live in peace.

Garbage dumps provide a ready meal for scavenging animals and warmth for some small animals to breed.

Parks and gardens contain a variety of habitats, from grass and trees to hedges and flower beds.

Fresh water in towns, from rivers or streams to garden ponds, reservoirs and gravel pits, provide an ideal habitat for all kinds of plants and animals.

Wildlife is not difficult to find in towns and cities, even in the most built-up areas. Some plants can even survive in the cracks between paving stones, and some birds are as happy to nest on building ledges as on sea cliffs.

Remember that most of the plants and animals that you find will have moved into the urban area from the surrounding countryside. A town with plenty of water, grass, and trees will obviously attract a greater variety of wildlife than one with little vegetation. Look out, too, for exotic species from other countries.

kestrel

London plane tree

honey bee

ox-eye daisy

gray squirrel

red campion

garden tiger moth caterpillar

goldeneye duck

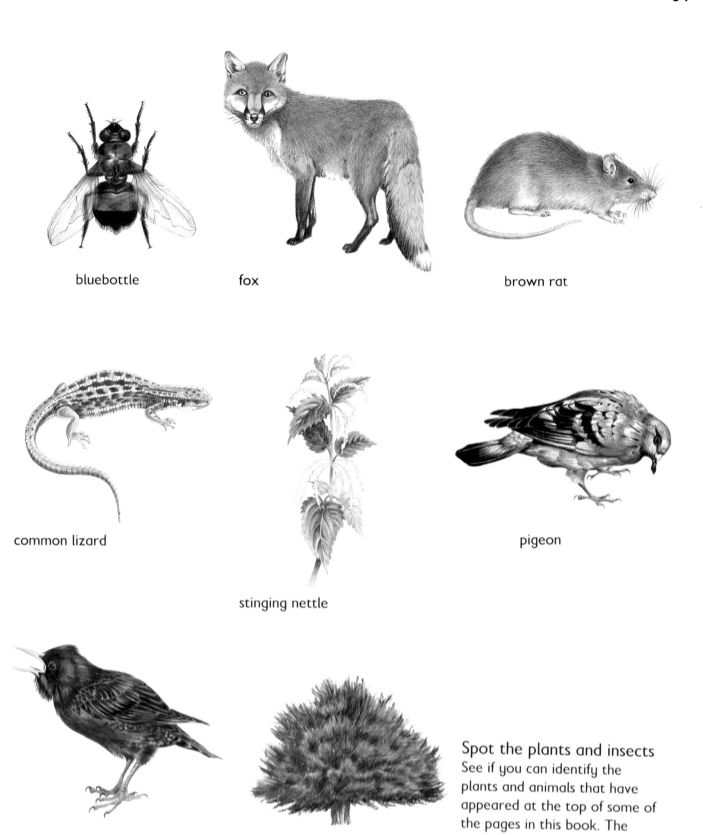

bluebottle

fox

brown rat

common lizard

stinging nettle

pigeon

starling

yew

Spot the plants and insects
See if you can identify the plants and animals that have appeared at the top of some of the pages in this book. The answers are on the next page.

Answers to quiz: p2 stinging
nettle, p3 brown rat, p5 common
lizard, p6 ox-eye daisy, p9 garden
tiger moth caterpillar, p11 yew,
p13 goldeneye duck, p15 gray
squirrel, p17 red campion,
p19 bluebottle, p21 pigeon,
p23 kestrel, p24 starling,
p27 London plane tree, p29 fox,
p32 honey bee.

PRINTED IN BELGIUM BY

INTERNATIONAL BOOK PRODUCTION